Poetry In Motion

Amanda Gail Click
"Mandy"

Edited By
Marilyn Ruth Burke

Illustrations By
Alexandrea Dioso; Makati City, Philippines
Christina Coy, Salem, Oregon - Layout Artist
Darryl Kim Natividad, Los Baños, Philippines
Jeash Coven Mizpah Del A. Artajo; Bayawan, Philippines
Katarina Lazic, Nis, Serbia
Mohamad Alm, Cairo, Egypt
Mohammad Sazzad Hossain Khan, Dhaka, Bangladesh
Paras Bhalodiya, Surat, India
S.M Nazmul Hasan, Dhaka, Bangladesh

Published By
Angelina College

Net proceeds from the sale of this book will benefit the East Texas Fun Bunch Scholarship Fund at Angelina College in Lufkin, Texas - 170(c)(1)

Library of Congress Control Number: 2019915549
ISBN 978-1-7342507-0-1

Special Thanks to Cliff Pelloni of Idea to Author Publishing
www.IdeatoAuthor.net

Published By
Angelina College

The carefree butterflies on the cover
of this book represents
celebration
endurance and expansion
freedom
gracefulness
hope
individuality
life
playfulness and profound change
renewal and responsibility and romance
spirituality
transformation and transition
vibrant joy

REMEMBER:
Mandy, you and I have endless opportunities,
potential and possibilities
to emerge into a new life waiting for us...
to set aside everything that is known to us
and
to embrace a new way of being
And so, it is...
With love, laughter, and Light,
Marilyn

Mandy is donating the net proceeds from the sale of this book to benefit the:

East Texas Fun Bunch Scholarship Fund at
Angelina College
170(c)(1)

The East Texas Fun Bunch Scholarship was established to support adults with intellectual and developmental disabilities (I/DD) and related conditions. This scholarship helps students participate in community services courses, including, but not limited to fine arts, technology, sign language and communications, kinesiology and others. In addition, the scholarship will fund rush tickets for a parent, guardian, staff member, or significant other to accompany ETFB students attending Angelina Arts Alliance performances and Angelina College athletic events on campus.

Preference is for adults who reside in Angelina County and live in a retirement/nursing home facility, participate in a sheltered/ vocational workshop or maintain the services of a mental health and developmental disability services provider. Through the Community Services Division, the teachers will come to the workshop and/or facility to teach the students.

If you want more information about the ETFB Scholarship Fund and/or want to make an additional donation, please contact:

Scholarship Coordinator
Angelina College
3500 S 1st St
Lufkin, Texas 75901-7328
936.633.4545
OR
Please make all checks payable to:
Angelina College, and in the memo section write:
ETFB Scholarship Fund
MAIL TO:
Angelina College
Scholarship Fund
P.O. Box 1768
Lufkin, Texas 75902-1768

Excellent
Time
For
Bonding

iii

Acknowledgements

I am dedicating this book to the following people (listed in alphabetical order according to their first name). They have all been good, kind and supportive of me all of these years. They looked out for me. They always helped me when I needed the help. They have always loved me whenever I needed to be comforted or needed a hand to hold. I appreciate all of them every day of my life. I want to thank God that they will always be in my heart.

Andrea Grimes
Art and Karen Nelson
Cheryl Woolf Sims
Elton McCune
Emily Hart
Galan Baugh Click (my Mom)
Gary Delaune
James (Jim) M. Wong
Jan Massey
Jeanne Fullerton
JoAnn Patterson
Kathy Manley
Laura Elizabeth Edmundson (my sister)
Marilyn Ruth Burke
Mark and Regina Mayberry
Matthew Moseley
My friends and staff at First Baptist Church Lufkin
My friends and staff at the Gateway Community Partners, Inc.
        Workshops in both Jacksonville and Lufkin, Texas
My friends and staff at the Rusk workshop (prior to its closing)
Pam Trotty
Robby and Laurie Hefner
Sylvia Dominey
Teresa Kyle
Tina Shafer Osburn
Vernay Carrington

This book is also in memory of the following people who are deceased. I want to thank them for being in my life. I miss them so much.
They were so sweet to me. They are now in Heaven, and they are very much loved by Jesus.

Beth Cannon, Freddy Cudjo, Jerry Chandler, Linda Delaune, Tammy Minchew,
    Doyle Click (my Grandfather) and JoAnn Click (my Grandmother)

Foreword

The Greek word for "poet" is *poiētēs*, meaning "to make." Creating poetry involves expressing the human condition or emotions through the combination of ordinary words using a rhyme scheme, meter or rhythm, and word sounds. Ms. Click's poetry addresses themes of faith, friendship, grief, and love from her unique lived experience. I first encountered Ms. Click's poetry because of her participation with the *East Texas Fun Bunch*, Inc. which was a local organization serving people with developmental disabilities from 2010 - 2017. In Ms. Click's poem entitled "Fun Bunch" she writes:

Comforting and caring for our friends and bonding are what we do,
To make us brighter, happier, and make our hearts so kind and true.

I suspect most people will resonate with the joy of finding friends whose hearts are kind and true. Angelina College is proud to support the East Texas Fun Bunch Scholarship Fund, and values the relationships AC students in the Human Services program develop with the Fun Bunch members. The College is grateful that the proceeds from the sale of "Poetry In Motion" will benefit the East Texas Fun Bunch scholarship program at Angelina College, and that the book is available in the AC Campus Store.

I hope you enjoy the book as much as I did.

Dr. Michael J. Simon
President
Angelina College

v

A Note From The Author

My name is Amanda Gail Click. I was born December 18, 1976 in Rusk, Texas. I was raised in Alto, Texas by my parents Eddie and Galan Click of Alto. I am 43 years of age now! I started school in Alto in 1981 and graduated May 31, 1996. I was not the most popular in my class, but I was always fond of writing words down on paper when I started junior high school!

I had a tough time in school making new friends and I never did fit in. I was painfully shy and less talkative when I was around people! I was always hiding inside my shell and never wanted to come out. One year in 1999, I got my picture in the newspaper because I wrote a poem about a special friend of mine passing away!

I started writing poems after I got out of high school because I had so many feelings bottled up inside of me that I needed to let them out! So I decided to take a sheet of paper and writing pen and write down how I was feeling! All those feelings came from me bottled up inside my shell all those years in school and sometimes at home. I thought that poetry and a journal would help me release out of my shell!

I was less talkative and outgoing when I was writing my poems years ago! I now work at a workshop in Lufkin, Texas with mentally challenged adults! I enjoy it!! Now I am more opened up to people, more talkative, and out of my shell more! I feel like they have helped me over all these years with managing my feelings, dealing with them, and being more outgoing! I am proud of myself for that!

I have favorite things that I like! They are purses, clothes, makeup, and jewelry. Nowadays, I go out more with my friends, and work everyday, and in my spare time at home, I watch TV, play games, and just do nothing! I am one lucky person! I don't do much in my life, but that's just the way it is! I can't go into details about how many poems I have written from 1998 to 2019! With gratitude,

Amanda Gail Click

"Mandy"

GATEWAY
Community Partners
1305 Tulane Dr., Lufkin, Texas 75902

Table Of Contents

Chapter 5 — FRIENDS

Chapter 6 — GRIEF

Chapter 7 — HOLIDAYS

Chapter 8 — LOVE

Chapter 9 — NATURE

Chapter 10 — WEATHER

Chapter 1
CAMP and ETFB

Lakeview Methodist Conference Center
Palestine, Texas

ETFB - East Texas Fun Bunch, Inc. A 501(c)(3) Organization
(Excellent Time For Bonding) 2010-2017
Founded By
Marilyn Ruth Burke, Director
James M. Wong, Secretary/Treasurer
Successors were: Directors: Kathy J. Manley and Pam Trotty
Secretary/Treasurer: Jeanne Fullerton

EAST TEXAS
FUN
BUNCH

Lakeview Camp

Lakeview Camp was so very fun,
With all of the beautiful weather,
and sunshiny days.
Camp was the place we spent time
With our friends,
And cherished memories for always.
We did all kinds of dancing and sang
Songs,
That were the music of our hearts.
We had fun as we stayed together.
Arts and crafts were also fun.
We enjoyed making keychains
That will be our treasure that we will remember
Forever.
All of the games we played,
We won trophies, candy,
And stuffed animals.
They were so soft and loveable.
Friends like us enjoyed ourselves.
We walked around,
Looking at the blue sky,
So beautiful and bright,
And looked at heaven as it gave
Us light.
We looked at the beautiful lake,
And went on a long walk.
The lake was as pretty as the sun,
And was as beautiful as heaven.

Going to church was also fun, too.
We sang songs and worshipped the Lord
And talked about all of God's beautiful
Things.
Basketball and volleyball were
The sports that we loved to play.
We enjoyed Lakeview Camp
In every friendly way.
We went to the gift shop and bought
Souvenirs for ourselves, and for other friends.
We were the friends down there
Who always like to love, give and share.
Lakeview Camp was fun for us
When we were there.
While we were roasting marshmallows around
The camp fire,
We had some delicious s'mores.
Lakeview Camp is the place where we have fun,
Get together,
And enjoy the sweetest days.
When we go back to Lakeview Camp,
We will have our friends with us,
And enjoy ourselves
In many friendly ways.

Amanda Click
April 30, 2001

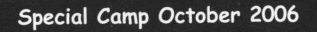

Special Camp October 2006

All my friends at special camp
were very sweet
with all their smiling
faces.
The fun we had at special camp
was arts and crafts
and looking at beautiful
places.
The most beautiful places
were the camp fire
and the lake.
The camp fire was beautiful
at night,
and seeing the stars
in the sky,
showing off their beautiful
light.
Fishing was fun with the lake
and its beautiful
water ,
gently flowing.

4

Flowing within God's heart.
We always stayed close
to each other,
and we will never be apart.
The prayer boxes we made
were God's Bible.
A Bible full of prayers
that brought us friendship
and love.
Special camp was so exciting
that we were all in God's
hands from above.
The counselors reached out to
all of us
whenever we needed a hand.
They were our angels
who watched over us
and our guardians
who always understand.
All the memories we had with us
at special camp,
will stay with us
and stay in our hearts
forever.
The more we go to special camp
and see our friends,
the more we will keep
our hearts together.

By: Amanda Click
October 31, 2006

A SPECIAL THANKS TO MS. TERESA KYLE
FROM ALL OF US AT GATEWAY
and THE EAST TEXAS FUN BUNCH

We all just want to thank you so much
for your help so sweet and dear.
You are always our angel and
you are always near.

Every day when we think of you,
we love and miss you.
Looking at your sweet face,
you've touched our hearts in many ways.
Ms. Teresa, you are in our memories and
in our prayers on the sweetest days.

We will also pray for your mom
who is doing okay and hanging in there.
Holding you tenderly in our arms,
we will always show you how much we care.

Ms. Teresa, we love you and your mom
who is always your angel from above.
We hope to come visit you one day,
give you a hug and fill your heart with love.

You are our special friend.
We will always love you til the end.

Photo courtesy of Lufkin Daily News
Lufkindailynews.com
November 28, 2014 (page 1a)

By Mandy Click
August 14, 2015

FOR: MS. VERNAY CARRINGTON
AND EVERYONE AT THE EAST TEXAS FUN BUNCH

Ms. Vernay,
I just want to
say,
that you are
our favorite
friend and
sweet angel
in every
special way.
We always enjoy ringing
handbells,
and singing a sweet,
beautiful song,
it makes my heart fill
with joy
all day long.
You are always glowing,
with the love in
your heart,
and a smile on your
face.
Thank you for being a part
of us and working
with us.
You are so blessed to have
us everyday,
as we ring our bells,
get together,
and pray.
You are always there with
us in God's
sweet, heavenly
place.

BY MANDY CLICK
ON SEPTEMBER 27, 2015

WE ALL LOVE YOU,
AND MAY GOD BLESS
YOU

The East Texas Fun Bunch

Friendly ways of sharing our joy
For every girl and boy.

Unique and fun ideas everyday
Make the sun shine in every way.

Nice faces and sweet smiles fill
Our hearts with friendship and love,
And God's angels from Heaven above.

Best friends love and trust one another
and always care and bond with each other.

Usually we have so much fun being together,
And hold onto all of our great memories we have forever.

Nice and friendly angels are always here on the sweetest days.
They are my angels who shine with me in every way.

Comforting and caring for our friends and bonding are what we do,
To make us brighter, happier, and make our hearts so kind and true.

Having fun is what it's all about;
All of my friends
All of my angels,
Always look up to me so sweet and dear
Forever in our memories and in
Our hearts, the East Texas Fun Bunch
Is why we are here.
Friendly Hearts   Friendly Places and Faces

Elizabeth   Billy
Kathy,   Cornelius
Kayla   Jason
Mandy   Jim
Rochelle   Nickolas
Teresa   Tracy

Fun With My Friends At - ETFB

Sharing times
with my friends at ETFB,
Caring for the ones
I love,
and the faces that I see,
I enjoy all of my angels,
singing and laughing
together,
and having fun with me.
Hanging out with my friends
at ETFB,
Looking into their sweet faces
of heaven
and the light,
they have a heart to love
and a beautiful smile from
heaven above
so pretty and bright

by Mandy Click
on December 1, 2014

Carnival Ecstasy Cruise
January 13-17, 2011

First ETFB/AC Computer Graduation Class:
Thursday, February 12- March 26, 2015

9

To: Ms. Cheryl Woolf Sims
Goodbye and Farewell

My friend,
Ms. Cheryl, I want
to say
Thank you for
having me and teaching
me in music class
on Thursday.
I just want to say
farewell
and goodbye
I do miss and love you
so much,
there's no need to
cry
You were the best
to me
You were true to my
heart and my sweet friend
who I trusted right
from the start.
I enjoyed the hand bells
that I played,
they sounded
wonderful;

10

The music that you
played for
me,
it was so sweet and
beautiful.
Some Thursdays
when we sang along
to Amazing Grace,
you lifted me
up
and put a smile
On my face.
Angels were always
at my side giving me
wings of love.
Ms. Cheryl, you give me joy to my heart
and you're blessed
to have me as your friend.
I will miss you
so very
very much.
You will be one of my
fond memories
until the
end.
by Mandy Click
Written on November 16, 2017
(Thursday)

11

12

Chapter 2

CHURCH

Healing Prayer:
Angel Stone & Healing Prayer

Just hold this
precious stone close to your
heart,
It is a reminder
of your healing prayers
and your embrace in God's
love.
The heavenly angel on this
stone
is very beautiful,
and glowing like the stars
in heaven above.
When you look at this stone,
it will fill your heart with
warmth,
and protect you with its
guiding light.
An angel as pretty as this
one,
is holding a cross
of faithfulness and love,
like heaven that is beautiful
and bright.
Holding this precious stone
in the palm of your
hand,
there is an angel who loves
you,
protects you,
and guides your heart safely
to a friend who will
understand.

14

Healing Prayer ——

"I will always be there
and keep you safe in my heart
and make sure the goodness
of friendship stays together
and never part.
I am your angel full of light
and love.
You are always my friend who
has a trusting heart from above.
Forever and for always,
you are in my heart in every way.
The healing prayer stone,
so sweet,
so lovely,
is the healing of your heart
every sweet day."

By: Mandy Click
April 22, 2009

Lord, Please Help Me

Lord, help me get through all my troubles
with an angel watching over me.
Give me all the loving I need
and the beautiful heavens that I see.
Give me the strength to live and
breathe.
I love you Lord and you are easy
to believe.
If something ever happens to me,
you can guide and protect me
from danger.
Lord, you are the one I trust
for always,
with a sweet thank you in many
sweet ways.
Lord, I know you are up in heaven
looking down at me
and loving me.
When something terrible happens to me,
I am really sensitive about it, Lord.
You can wipe my tears away
and make me feel better about things,
with love and happiness that
a good life brings.
If I ever need you, Lord, I will let
you know.
If I am ever in trouble about anything
or anybody, I will come to you
and you can make my flowers grow.

Mandy
October 16, 1999

16

My Prayer In God's Hands

"Oh, Lord, may I take your hand
and walk with you in the light of
heaven.
There will be no pain,
no sorrow,
and no tears.
There will be happiness
and joy throughout your years.
Lord,
I love you so
with your halo,
and your wings
All aglow.
Lord, you will forever be blessed,
and my heart
will always be in your
hands.
I love you Lord."

Amen

By: Amanda Click
October 31, 2006

To: God
With Love and Support

There may come a
time in my life
when I need
Love and support from
you,
whenever I am lonely,
whenever I am blue,
You are always
there with me,
when the sunset starts
to fade away,
and nighttime begins
to fall.
So full of support and
love,
I will hear your sweet
voice call.
You have always been
my shelter from the
storm
since the day I was
born into your
heart.
Staying with you,
we will never be worlds
apart.
God,
you will take
care of me,
like my mama,
and my sister.
They always bring out
the best in me,
when I look at God's
heavenly sky that
I see.

God,
there is one thing
that I want
to say,
that I love you
and you are very special
to me
in every way.
God,
I am thankful
for all your living
things,
myself,
my family,
and my friends.
I am blessed
to have
your guidance,
your support,
your love and
your beautiful angels
from heaven
above.
I want to be the arms
that hold you
and caress you,
when the storm blows
away,
and the raindrops melt
away.
Everyone loves me
and trusts me,
like you do.
Your sweet love for
me is so kind
and so true.

By Mandy Click
May 1, 2011

19

When Angels Weep

There is a sky so beautiful and blue for all angels
who weep and shed a tear.
Their wings give them the strength to love,
to heal, and kiss away their fears.
Angels are pretty and full of light,
but when angels weep,
their tears fall like the rain on a beautiful night.
Whenever the tough times get to them,
they let light from God shine on their wings,
making them feel stronger and have a heart to love
on all beautiful things.
When angels weep, they kiss the pretty blue sky
with shining stars,
and stay up in heaven where they fly.
To keep their tears from falling, they catch a falling
star,
and be heaven-sent from where they are.
An angel's love is much sweeter than the gloomy
clouds above.
Their halos give them peace and harmony,
warming their hearts tenderly with precious, friendly love.

Amanda Click

Chapter 3

COLORS

Rainbows That Shine Like Gold

The rainbows that shine like gold are
full of pretty colors.
Rainbows are as pretty as the clear,
blue sky.
They stay pretty so that angels can glance
at them as they fly.
Angels like to wish on a rainbow when they shine
like gold.
When they fly across the rainbow, they always share
their sweet love together to have
and to hold.
A color that would go with an angel, would
be the color gold, a color
that will make their wings beautiful in
the light.
Angels have a feeling of love by their side
when the rainbow shines bright.
Their wings shine with them everyday.
Rainbows are pretty like the sunshine, the big,
blue sky, the flowers, and the stars in
every way.
All of these pretty things belong in the sky,
while the angels dream about them.
Angels like the soft colors like pink, lavender,
blue, and pale yellow; the colors they
need to make them strong.
In heaven, angels like to watch the rainbow
as it brightens the sky and sing a love song.
They sing songs about loving, caring, and sharing,
day and night.
When angels fall asleep and dream at night,
they dream of the rainbows that shine
like gold in the sunlight.
Love is so strong that they look at a pretty rainbow.
A rainbow full of pretty colors they love
and their beautiful wings that glow.

Mandy
October 2, 1999

Silver And Gold

Silver and gold are pretty colors.
They are like the stars in
the sky,
and the love that shines
beautifully in heaven up high.
Silver and gold looks good
on a diamond ring.
It shows all the beauty and
sparkle that it brings.
Silver and gold are two colors
that are very bright.
They are so pretty in the light.
The colors of the rainbow are
very nice like silver and gold.
Angels love their halos silver and gold
with ribbons and flowers.
They are the most pretty colors
in heaven that will stay.
Silver and gold are an
angel's best colors, and
they shine on their wings.
On a pretty spring day,
silver and gold will make
the angels glow,
and the pretty flowers grow.

Mandy

When I Catch A Rainbow

When I catch a rainbow with you,
you are my special friend so kind and true.
As the rainbow shines so bright,
I will think of you in the heavenly light.
It is so sweet when we wish on a star together.
The rainbow is a friendly love that will
last forever.
When I catch a rainbow of friendship
and love,
I will catch it and the stars for the both of us,
when we look at heaven above.
You are my friend so nice when the rainbow of
friendship shines with its beautiful colors.
We are friends who write each other letters
and share,
and we are best buddies who dream of love,
friendship, and care.
We hold on to each other,
if our hearts are aching,
and our souls are breaking.
We have the rainbow watching over us like
the light of day.
The love of friendship will stay with us
and never take us away.
The best part of friendship is love.
A love that will keep us looking at the rainbow
in the heavens above.
Friends like us give warm hugs and sweet dreams,
and that shows us what friendship really means.
The rainbow we see shines really beautiful
in the pretty blue sky.
If we are going through the darkest days,
our hearts will have wings to fly.
When I catch a rainbow with you,
you will always be my friend.
You will always be so faithful and true
to me until the end.

Mandy

Chapter 4

FAMILY

Laura

I just want to thank
you
for being my sister
and my best friend.
You will always be
until the
end.
You mean so much to
me
and you are my every
thing.
I'm very blessed to have
you in my life,
and in my heart.
Thinking of you everyday;
you are special to me in
every way.
You are a sister who I can
always count on
forever.
We get along so good
that I always think about
the times
we share together.
My heart is an open door
for you
whenever you need me for
anything.
You are an angel to me who
has wings,
so pretty and full of light,
and a halo so beautiful
and bright

26

there is one thing I want
to say sis,
any sweet day,
that I love you
and that you have a heart
so kind,
so true.

From Your Sister,
Mandy Click

Mother

Mother, you are my gift from God,
And my light of love.
Angels like you are so sweet,
From heaven above.
You are my beauty that will never die,
And as beautiful as the clear blue sky.
Mother,
Just think of me,
And I will give you a smile,
So sweet and so beautiful to see.
Forever,
I will love you,
No matter what.
You are my sunshine so sweet and true.
Mother,
Love is where my heart is,
For always.
You are my pretty flower and my best friend
Who is always there for me,
On my darkest days.
Mother,
You will always be in my heart
And in my soul, forever.
You are the sweetest, and most trusting woman,
Ever

Amanda Click

Chapter 5

FRIENDS

A Special Friend

There is one true person in my heart,
and a love so sweet that will never be apart.
That is my special friend,
who will always love me until the end.
I always write her letters and they fill her heart
with the friendliest love.
She is one good, trusting person so sweet
like the heavens above.
In her heart, love will always be there,
with tender love and care.
This special friend is my shining star that will never
fade away.
She will always be in my heart to stay.
This sweet poem is to my special friend so sweet
with love to share,
and a special friend who will always be there.
This is a friend who I trust so sweet and dear
and a love so near.

Her name is Jan.
Mandy

Friend

Friend, you are so special.
You are so nice and sweet,
and a person who is very neat.
You are a friend so trusting
and confident.
A friend like you is very intelligent
and very smart.
You are a friend who will always be there,
and someone who will always care.
I like to have a friend like you,
who is very faithful and true.
Thanks for being my friend,
and being so nice to me.
Friendship will always stay with you,
Forever.

Mandy

Come To Me

Whenever you are feeling weak,
and need to feel better,
I will comfort you and make you strong.
Come to me,
hold on to me,
and I will safely guide my love
into your heart.
With my arms around you,
love will never be apart.
If your world is turning cold,
and your heart is out of control,
I will make things bloom into your heart,
like the pretty flowers that grow,
and the blue moon that glows.
Come to me,
hold on to me,
and I will let your tears stop falling.
With a sweet, friendly hug,
I will always love you.
Don't worry, sweet dreams are always
there to come true.
I understand how you are feeling now.
I will help you find a way out of your hurting
somehow.
Come to me,
hold on to me,
and I will guide and protect you with
my love.
As long as you feel better and the love in your
heart never ends,
angels will be watching you from heaven
above.
Come to me,
hold on to me,
and please tell me,
Will the pretty blue sky ever shine on you?
Will the love in your heart get rid of the pain
that you are going through?
Just hold on to me, and I will make everything
go away.
I love you, and love will always shine
on your darkest days.

ANYTHING

Anything that comes to mind,
anything that I want to write down,
anything that I am thankful for,
anything that my family and friends need;
they are always very loyal, sweet, and kind!
This is my journal,
this is my life;
my thoughts,
my feelings,
my family and friends who will
never let me down.
You will always see a smile,
never a frown!
Anything that drowns me in fear
I will let go,
and I won't shed a tear!
My heart will be strong,
and it will never ache.
It will never be broken,
and it won't be hard to take!
Anything that makes me feel comfortable,
secure and easy
is what I want from God,
so I won't get back in my shell!
There are secrets from my past
I will not tell!
Anything that I want from God,
like comfort, serenity, and love,
will be from my family and friends,
and my Heavenly Father sent from above!
I will always remember
anything that comes to mind
will never let me down!
You will always see a smile;
never a frown!

WRITTEN BY: AMANDA CLICK **33**

Friends

Friends always mend broken hearts,
And heal us with a beauty
That will never die.
Friends comfort us with love
Unconditionally if we need tears
To cry.
Friends are a heart of gold,
When we need a loved one to hold.
Friend are always sweet,
When we give them a gift.
Friends are always there when we
Need a lift.
Having friends is like having feelings
Of love.
If we ever lose a friend,
They will be in heaven above.
Friends warm our hearts and souls,
And make us feel better.
The kindest thing you can do is write
Them a friendly letter.
Friends make us feel alive.
They will always be hearts of
Our lives.

Amanda Click

I'm Not Alone

I'm not alone, therefore I have love in my heart.
The love is strong in my heart that it will
never be apart.
I will always have a friend beside
if something does not go right.
I'm not alone as long I look at angels
in the light.
Everything is going to be alright as long as
love doesn't fade away.
My heart will not break and I am not alone
with someone by my side for always.
I have friends who are forgiving, sweet
and who have feelings for me.
They will be there to wipe away my tears,
and help me calm my fears.
If something goes wrong, I know that my heart
will break.
Tough times and troubles are the hardest
thing to take.
If I'm not alone, my love won't make
me blue.
The angels are making sure I'm always
okay and everything stays sweet and true.
Love takes time to heal,
and feelings are there to feel.
I will be okay as long as I'm not alone,
and all of the bad, hurtful feelings in my
heart will be gone.

Mandy
April 15, 2000

My Heart

My heart is always full of friendship
and trust.
It is my foundation and it is my
life.
Happiness is what
matters to me,
as long as I lighten up and look
at the pretty blue
sky
that I see.
My heart feels calm
and full of strength
on a beautiful day,
but whenever someone gets on
my case about something,
tears and disappointment get
in my way.
My heart feels
happy and satisfied when
I turn to a friend.
A love so strong
and so moving
is a love that will never
come to an end.
I have got teased a lot
by others in the past,
and it has made my heart
carry on.
I try not to think back to
the past,
but sometimes my heart
just can't help it.
I know deep down
in my heart that I
can hold back tears
when I feel like I am

going to cry.
Sometimes I can't help it if I don't
say much
and I feel shy.
I try not to be,
and my heart makes
sure of that.
I have a boyfriend who loves me,
and keeps me in line.
He makes sure that my heart is
okay.
Forever,
he will always be mine.
My heart has been really
sensitive
and whenever it is feeling
blue, I go to a
friend to heal the
wounds,
and that makes my heart feel
better.
My friends are the angels I
look up to,
when my heart is falling
apart.
I know that today will not
be the last of all days, so
my heart will stay strong.
Life is too short for my heart
to worry about anything.
My heart will be relieved
and not have a broken wing.
With my heart
always staying alive,
I know I will survive.

Mandy Click
December 15, 2005

My One True Friend

You are my one true friend,
who will always depend on me
and trust me until the end.
You are my friend who makes me feel
better when I am feeling down.
You are so sweet that you are fun to be around.
Love is the feeling we need in our hearts
when we are together.
A friend like you is so special, so sweet,
and precious forever.
Friend, I promise you that I will never
leave you.
I don't know what I would do without you,
by my side.
Your tender smile reminds me of how
we laughed and cried.
I will always trust you with love in your heart,
and I will take care of you,
and I will never let our friendship
fall apart.
Having a friend like you always knows how
I feel,
and who will always comfort me if I am hurting
real bad and give me the strength to heal.
You are my one true friend who will
always wipe my tears away.
You will always be in my heart to stay.

Mandy

PRAY FOR ME

Through the storm,
Through the rain,
Your open arms will caress me,
And will shelter me in your shade.
With a beautiful rainbow,
So pretty,
So bright,
Your light for me in heaven
Will never fade.
Through the steps of your stairway
That lead me to you heart,
Through the love and friendship
That will never be apart;
You are always there with me
In God's precious name.
When the rains pour down
and the waves crash around,
I will always feel safe
In your loving arms,
And in your loving hands.
Hands of fulfillment,
Hands of support,
Hands that heal my heart
When it is in pain.
Having friends is the most
Precious thing ever.
Whenever you find my heart hurting,
Pray for me
And you will see that we will
Always be friends forever.
In God's precious name,
He will take you to a heavenly place.
I love you,
Cherish you,
And trust you.

To: Matthew Joseph Moseley "Matty"
From: Mandy Click

THE ORNAMENT OF LOVE

The ornament of love is a symbol
of friendship from heaven above.
It is a gift from an angel in heaven,
with all the pretty colors of the sunset,
and all of the pinks, yellows, and oranges.
The ornament of love shows us how to
make friends and have feelings for
one another.
It lets us love and care for each other.
It helps us get rid of all the bad feelings
and releases the hurt and pain
in our hearts.
This ornament of love will heal our broken hearts
and get rid of the tough times in every sweet way.
Forever, as we look into this precious ornament
of love,
we will be saved by angels every day.

MANDY

The Seeds Of Life

Friends,
they are the seeds of life
growing into a beautiful
bouquet of flowers.
When we have friends
around us,
it is like having a cool,
gentle breeze
whispering through
the air.
When we need a hug
or a shoulder to cry on,
friends will always
be there.
On beautiful days,
rain or shine,
friends show us how
much they care

By: Mandy Click
on May 25, 2009

TO MY GOOD FRIEND

Thank you for being such a nice person to me.
You are my friend who I can trust, always,
And keep my heart strong on
My sweetest days.
I just want you to know,
That you are just a friend,
So kind and so sweet,
And for all of the friendliness
That you show.
Keep me in your heart, friend
For who I am,
And for who I will always be.
From now until I've known you,
You have been close to my heart.
The feeling of friendship has kept me strong
And my heart will never break.
The love and friendship from you,
That is in my heart,
Will never be forgotten,
And will never fade away.
Friendship is love like a beautiful flower
That will stay alive and never wilt.
Friend, you bring out the very best in me
And forever in my heart,
Love will stay.

By: Amanda Click

What Do I Do

What do I do with my friends?
I hold them close to my heart,
with precious love that will never fall apart.

What do I do with my heart?
I make it feel better when its breaking,
and make love heal when its aching.

What do I do with my love?
I make it strong and very sweet in a precious
way,
and watch it shine in heaven on a
beautiful sunny day.

What do I do with my soul?
I do whatever is good for it day and night,
look at beautiful things and make
everything alright.

What do I do with my friendliness?
I share it with a best friend,
and keep it in my heart
until the end.

Mandy

43

TAMMY MINCHEW
JERRY CHANDLER
FREDDY CUDJO
BETH CANNON
LINDA DELAUNE
DOYLE CLICK
JOANN CLICK

Chapter 6

GRIEF

All The Love Is Gone

All the love is gone,
for there are tears falling
from my eyes.
Tears that are full of pain,
are running down my face
like the pouring rain.

All the love is gone,
and my heart is breaking.
When my feelings are aching,
I miss my best friends so bad,
like a crying face that is so sad.

All the love is gone,
and I need to try to move on.
I need someone to help me
be strong,
and to help me do no wrong,
like a sweet, easy going love song.

All the love is gone,
therefore, I don't know what to do.
All I have to try to do is deal with
the way I feel,
like the love in my heart
that needs to heal.

Amanda G. Click
April 22, 1999

Dying

Dying is a part of life for everyone,
But it can be very sad.
When we heal from someone passing away,
We would not feel so bad.
It could be a friend or a loved one
We miss forever.
It is hard to hide the hurt,
And the tears from not being together.
When someone passes away,
They will be an angel looking down.
It is so sad for them not to be around.
If a loved one dies, what is a person to do?
People who had loved ones who have died,
Found it very hard to make it through.

Amanda Click

Grandpa

I just want to
say
that you were a
good man,
that you were very
blessed,
and very loved,
always.
During your funeral
service,
I choked up
with the sadness I
felt,
the tears that I
cried,
with all of my loved
ones by my
side.
I prayed with my
family all
together,
and we looked
back on all of your
memories
you have had forever.
The picture of you
and your puppy dog
was the most
precious memory
ever.
You loved him
everyday.
You took care of him
in every sweet way.
When I looked at your
angelic face
sleeping in a very
beautiful place,
it was so hard to move
on.

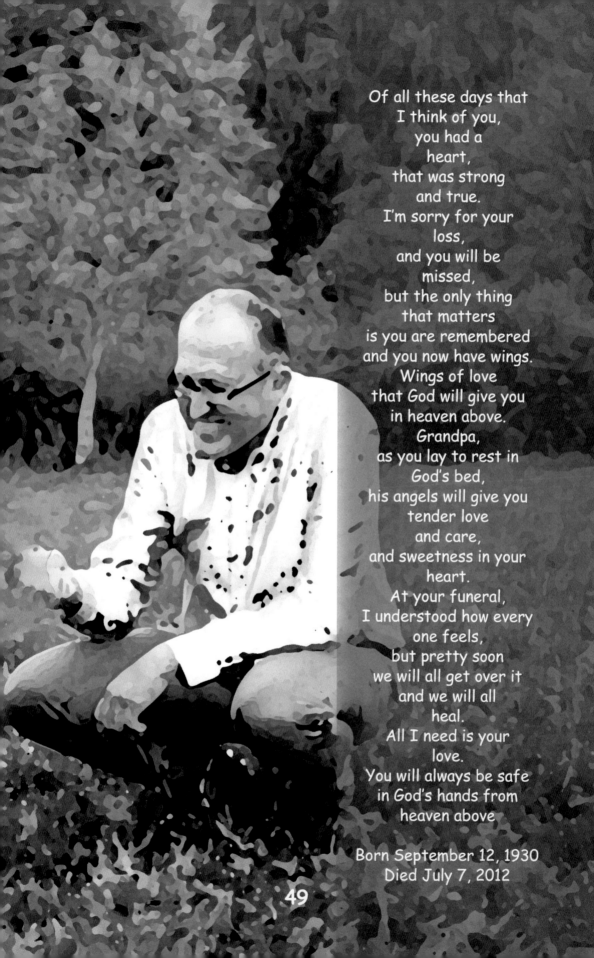

Of all these days that
I think of you,
you had a
heart,
that was strong
and true.
I'm sorry for your
loss,
and you will be
missed,
but the only thing
that matters
is you are remembered
and you now have wings.
Wings of love
that God will give you
in heaven above.
Grandpa,
as you lay to rest in
God's bed,
his angels will give you
tender love
and care,
and sweetness in your
heart.
At your funeral,
I understood how every
one feels,
but pretty soon
we will all get over it
and we will all
heal.
All I need is your
love.
You will always be safe
in God's hands from
heaven above

Born September 12, 1930
Died July 7, 2012

49

Healing The USA From The September 11th Tragedy

Healing the USA will take time
From this tragic day.
Hoping and praying is what we will do
To help millions and millions
Of innocent people precious lives
Have swept away.
God is watching the USA to make sure
It is going to be a safer place to live.
The hijackers that made the airplanes crash
Into the World Trade Center and the Pentagon
Were the ones that we will never trust
And never forgive.
Healing the USA is what we will do in order
To keep loved ones strong.
We are now wishing that these hijackers
Did not do us wrong.
The ones who lived,
Need a heart to love and a hand to hold.
The ones who died,

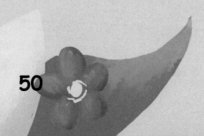

Their hearts have terribly weakened into
Deadly cold.
We love all people and their light of love.
They are our best friends that God sent us
From heaven above.
Looking at the USA flag,
Mourning and weeping,
We think of the people who died;
And we think of the colors,
Red, white, and blue.
These are the colors of freedom and patriotism
In our heart that will always
Be true.
God bless America,
To all families and friends.
Love will always be in our heart,
Getting rid of the pain and sadness
That will take time to end.

GOD BLESS AMERICA!
WE LOVE ALL PEOPLE!

It's Alright

It's alright, don't feel sad.
Your heart will heal.
Don't feel bad.

It's alright, don't cry.
Your tears and pain will go away.
Don't feel scared in any way.

It's alright, don't be scared.
Soon your heart will be filled with love.
Don't feel terrified, there are angels above.

It's alright, don't be alone.
I promise you, you will get well soon.
Don't be tearful, pretty soon your heart
will be filled with love as your very own.

It's alright, don't be worried.
You will be alright.
Don't feel lonely, there is the Lord watching
you in the light so beautiful and bright.

It's alright friend, you will survive.
Just hang in there.
Before long, you will feel better and be alive.

Mandy

Like The Rain

When my heart begins to hurt,
my tears fall like the rain,
leaving my soul to bleed and causing me pain.

If I ever have to deal with tough times,

I will have to hold on tighter to my faith, to live one more day.

Like the rain,
a thunderstorm rambles on when I lay in bed,
crying during the night.

One day,
I will settle down and watch the rain disappear,

giving me sunshine and beautiful light.

When the clouds cover the moon,

the rain will begin to fall.

With the sky so dark,
it is the stormiest night of all.

Like the rain,
the sunset sinks like a fallen tear.
I try to hold on to my heart
and make sure it is okay.

There is always an angel
watching over me in a heavenly
way.
One of these days,
there will be a rainbow hovering
over me to help me
make it through the rain
forget about the past,

and end the pain!

By: Amanda Click, 2003

Mourning The Loss Of Your Nephew

Baby, I know that you are taking it hard,
just thinking about your little angel
who has gone to heaven.
The loss of your nephew is very sad for you.
He will be there in heaven with the angels
full of light.
The light will shine on his precious face
as he lays to rest in God's hands,
with his beautiful wings shining bright.
I know that your heart is hurting,
and you are feeling the pain.

You mourned and you cried,
when your little nephew died,
and your heart was left in the rain.
Baby, I know that you miss your little angel,
and you are feeling the loss on a mourning day.
I have been feeling bad about your little nephew,
and all we need to do to feel better is to pray.
Angels like him always shine in heaven above.
He will always be in the light of heaven and in
God's love.

By: Mandy

SAVING OUR COUNTRY'S PEOPLE

A Heartbreaking Poem About The Recent Terrorist Attack Of The United States

The recent terrorist attack of the country is such a terrible,
Heartbreaking thing,
That it took the lives of people and their precious
Love away.
We can try to reach out to save the country's people
From this mournful tragedy
One sweet day.
These people are now hurting and their hearts are BREAKING.
We will soon save their lives so they will stop aching.
With tears running down and shocked looks
On our faces,
We know how these poor people feel,
With an angel watching over them,
It will take them time to heal.
All of the families with love ones,
Are now crying, carrying on, mourning,
And praying that they will be okay that they will
Survive.
We hope these people who have been hurt really bad
Will still be alive.
Something happening like this to our country's people
Is very heartbreaking and very tearful.
We will comfort these hurt people with our love and our strength,
And try to help them get rid of their loss and their fear.
We feel so sorry for their hurt and their pain.
Whoever started this tragedy is very pitiful and very insane.
We hope that there will be a way out of this tragedy.
Of this recent terrorist attack of the United States,
We hope people who survived will be comforted with tender
Love and care.

The United States is now affected after this horrific tragedy.
That these hurt people will need love and attention
And an angel who will always be there.
Love is what we need to save our country's people
And to save the severely sick who have special needs.
This terrorist attack of the United States
Is very inexplicable and is a real big mess,
And now we wish that this never took place.
The people who are still alive and well,
Are the ones who are very hurt, with tears running
Down their faces.
Maybe one sweet day,
Everyone will soon get better and will soon heal.
Letting go of the hurt will take time,
When these people are hurting and mourning
And knowing how they feel.
What will the world face in the near future,
After the loss of loved ones,
Losing faith and sympathy,
And shedding mournful tears?
With lots of grieving,
God bless America,
And hope that things will get better
Through the coming years.

Amanda Click

There Was Once A Little Girl

There was once a little girl that had no place
to go,
and had no one to protect her heart
and soul.
She was lost and all alone.
Without her mom and dad,
all the love was gone.
Her mom and dad ran away,
leaving her by herself without a place to stay.
She had a broken heart,
with all of the love torn apart.
This little girl needed someone to take
care of her and she needed lots of love.
Without the love,
there would be no one to save her from
heaven above.
As she looked into the darkness, she
wept and she cried,
thinking that all of her precious moments
and all of the love in her heart had died.
One day at home, she decided to call her
grandmother and talk to her about
how she felt.
So she decided to move in with her until
her heart healed.
Without her mom and dad it was kind
of hard for her to move on,
and for all the sweet loving memories
to be gone.

Her grandmother is now taking care of her
with all of the tender love and care.
Now she doesn't find it so hard to breathe
if someone is always there.
She feels better now with all of the love in
her heart and all of the strength in her soul.
Now the little girl and her grandmother
have many places to go,
like the long road that leads them to the love
and happiness that a precious life brings.
When they are together, they share all of their
precious things.
This little girl still misses her mom and dad.
She cannot figure out what happened
to them and why they ran off and left her
for so many days.
Now that the little girl has a place to live
and survive, the love in her heart will
be blessed in many ways.
Her grandmother will take care of her
and keep her alive,
with a strong heart and soul
and a place to survive.

Poem done by: Mandy
May 19, 2000

This poem was inspired by the song
"The Little Girl"
by John Michael Montgomery

The Tough Times

I can forget the tough times of the past,
put them behind me, and try not to think about
them any more,
but whenever the tough times come back to me,
I can cry when I need to and say what I feel.
It has been so long since I have cried about anything,
but so far,
I am okay.
There is always love in my heart to heal,
and there is always one sweet day when a friend can kiss
my tears away,
and keep them from running down my face.
I have been touched by an angel
from the most beautiful place.
If a loved one has passed away,
I could cry in the middle of the night,
like teardrops of rain falling from the midnight sky.
But so far, nothing like that has happened,
and so far, I've been strong.
Whenever there comes a day when I am not feeling
okay,
I can go to a friend and tell them what is wrong.
Love is so sweet when I have a friend to turn to,
when the tough times get to me.

Mandy

When I Feel Blue

When I feel blue, I feel the tears falling
from my eyes.
I feel my feelings being swept away,
and the rain falling on a
cloudy day.

When I feel blue, I feel the wind blowing
hard.
I feel the sky falling out of the blue,
and the flowers wilting with drops
of dew.

When I feel blue, I feel a stormy cloud
looking down on me.
I feel the snow making my heart cold,
and making me lonely with
no one to hold.

When I feel blue, I can make myself
feel better, looking at heaven and
its starry sky,
and an angel who will watch over
me and has wings to fly.

Mandy

When Teardrops Fall

When teardrops fall from my eyes,
it is you that I miss.
I love you so much that I
need a sweet, tender, and
loving kiss.
Love is such a sweet thing
and I don't want to shed
a tear.
I don't want to leave you,
because you are so sweet,
and so dear.
When teardrops fall, they fall
like the pouring rain.
My tears will give me a broken
heart and my feelings
will be full of pain.
I love you as my pretty flower
and my guardian angel who
is full of love.
You are the one who will heal
my tears and wipe
them away.
Forever, you will be my
sweetheart who will
love me everyday.
Your love is so sweet and so precious

that my tears will heal.
You will always love me
and you will protect my
feelings that I feel.
When teardrops fall, I always
think of you.
Whenever I miss you, it leaves
me feeling lonely and blue.
You are like the heavens that
are full of light.
When you are there with me,
I hold you tight all through
the night.
You will always have feelings for
me when my tears are full
of pain,
My heart will be strong and
not out in the pouring rain.
I love you so much that my
dreams will come true.
Whenever I am missing you,
I have tears in my eyes,
and forever in my heart,
I will always love you.

Mandy
March 16, 1999

While America Slept
Memories Of The 9-11 Terrorist Attacks

How did you feel on this September day,
when the whole city of New York blackened out
and drifted away?
Did you panic when the World Trade Center towers fell,
and watch people go through a living hell?
America slept silently when the towers burned up with everyone
inside making their way out,
and leaving the city with loved one dying in pain,
and screaming through the city out and about.
A big pile of smoke filled the clear, blue sky,
while pieces of the rubble blew up high,
taking New York City away.
People lost their loved ones and their freedom
as their belongings vanished into thin air on this September day.
Now that the Twin Towers are gone,
all that is left are memories of that day,
when the New Yorkers did not have the chance to be free.
The stars and stripes on the American Flag mean that we love
America from sea to shining sea.

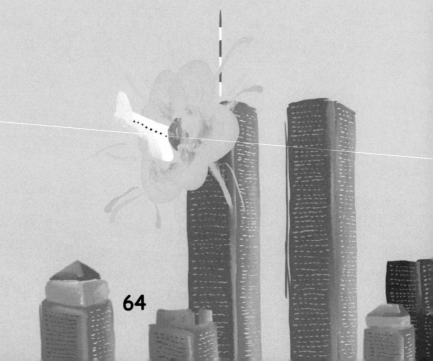

Words From A Poem Or A Song

A poem is a very beautiful
thing to write about, sometimes
good
and sometimes bad.
The words of a poem
or a song
can be words to strengthen
your heart
whenever you are feeling sad.
A song is words that can
be sung
and be said
with feeling deep in your heart,
so kind,
so true,
while reading a pretty poem can
relieve you
and heal you;
they often do.
They'll be happy songs that
make you feel loved
like an angel up high,
and they'll be sad songs that
make you feel empty
inside,
make you tear up,
and make you cry.
Words from a poem or a song
can touch your heart
whenever you feel torn
apart.
More than words can say,
one sweet day;
cry when you need to
and say what you
feel,
and words either from a
poem or a song
can make you
heal.

Mandy Click
January 18, 2010

65

Chapter 7

HOLIDAYS

New Year's Day 2000

New Year's Day is a time of celebrating with
Family and friends.
We share all of the good food, popping
Fireworks, and having parties together.
New Year's Day is a holiday we will celebrate
Forever.
Love and sharing require all of the fun on
This special holiday,
When we give warm hugs and strength in
Our hearts in every way.
The year 2000 is the year of the future
And a time of looking at the stars
On a clear night.
The future will always stay with us as
We celebrate this holiday with all the
Fireworks so beautiful and bright.
2000 will be a good year this
New Year's Day,
As we look into the new millennium.
Moments and memories of 1999 will
Always be remembered, as we celebrate
New Year's.
The year 2000 will stay with us for all of
The fun, laughter, and tears.

Mandy

Happy New Year's Day, Everyone!!

The Vase Of Flowers

The vase of flowers is very pretty
For any occasion.
They are very sweet to give as
A gift to a friend.
With a sweet thank you card,
They are very beautiful to send.
The vase of flowers is great for any occasion
For Christmas, Easter, or Valentine's Day.
These flowers always bloom with love
In every way.
Angels like these flowers that grow
In heaven in the beautiful light.
The vase of flowers looks as pretty
As the rainbow so beautiful and bright.

Mandy

Martin Luther King, Jr. Day

January 15, 2018 is when we celebrate Martin Luther
King, Jr. Birthday.
As we celebrate Martin Luther King, Jr's death
we remember him as the slain
civil rights leader.
There are many other things we remember
from this day in memory:
He broke onto the national civil rights scene in 1955;
He was one of the few social leaders;
He was in a 1960 mug shot,
and he began to speak out against the Vietnam War
and poverty.
Martin Luther King, Jr. died on April 4, 1968.
We will always remember Martin Luther King, Jr.
We will think of him and keep him in our
Memories.

Mandy

February

February is the month that we celebrate
Valentine's Day.
It is a month we cherish in every way.
We also celebrate Abraham Lincoln's birthday.
This month really puts joy in our hearts
and smiles on our faces,
and lets us look at the light in all
the beautiful places.
We like celebrating Valentine's Day
where we care for one another,
and love each other.
February is called the sweetheart month
of the year.
All of the angels like February with all
of the sharing of hearts, the laughter,
and the cheer.
We like all of the delicious candy, cookies,
chocolates, and conversation hearts
that are sweet.
Celebrating Valentine's Day is really neat.
The month of February will make all things
beautiful and bright,
and all of the angels celebrate Valentine's Day
in the beautiful light.

Mandy

To You, Valentine

Oh, my sweetheart,
you are my
light
you are my love!
Oh, my darling,
I will never
forget that
you love me
so!
I promise with
all my heart
that I will never
let you go!
I love you more
than you will
ever know!
Oh, my dear,
you brighten my
Valentine's Day with
your heart so close
to me, so near!
Oh, sweetie pie,
you always comfort me
and take my
pain away!
My heart always belong
to you on this
Sweet Valentine's Day!
To you, my Valentine,
To you, my true love,
you will forever
be mine!
From your secret admirer,

Mandy Click

The Easter Holidays

The Easter holidays are full of love and joy,
with its soft pastel colors,
like pink, purple, yellow, blue, green,
and orange.
Easter is all about hunting Easter
eggs and celebrating with family
and friends.
Easter's soft pastel colors are the
colors of caring, sharing, happiness
and love.
The Easter holidays are so full of
laughter and special surprises,
that Easter is a promise kept
forever,
and also the sweetest promise
with the sweetest love and wishes.
As Easter's soft pastel colors
beautifully brighten the
rainbow, they are the
colors of heaven.
The Easter holidays are the
beautiful Easter Lilies that
grow so pretty.
The Easter holidays are so
special in every way
and brightens the light everyday.
Forever in our hearts,
the Easter holidays are here to stay.

Mandy
April 1, 1999

Summertime

Summertime, summertime,
a day to run out in the soft, cool grass
everyday,
and enjoy vanilla ice cream in the hot
sunshine, in every way.
A day of summer fun is backyard barbecues
playing in the sand at the beach,
and having an ice-cold snowcone
to cool us down.
There are fireflies to catch on a long summer
night,
as we cup them in our hands and catch
their light.
Summertime is the time of the year we swim
in the swimming pool and do fun things,
and hear the beautiful sounds of nature
and the birds as they sing.
On hot summer nights we can camp out
and look at the stars, so very bright,
when the sunset and the heavens are a beautiful sight.
Summertime is a day of picking blackberries and flying
kites up in the big, blue sky,
and looking at the brightness and sunshine
up high.
Summertime, summertime,
what a time of the year we love,
and the hot summer days to cool us off
from heaven above.
Oh, we are so glad summertime is here.
It will bring us lots and lots of fun
all year.

Mandy
June 1, 2000

74

Thanksgiving

Thanksgiving is the holiday when we give
thanks and be with our family.
It is the time when families get together
and have Thanksgiving dinner,
like turkey and dressing, cranberry sauce,
and pumpkin pie.
Dinner on Thanksgiving is really nice
to enjoy,
with all the joy on sweet faces and the
hearts filled with all the love.
The month that goes with this holiday
is the month of November when the weather
is cooler and the leaves fall on
the ground.
Thanksgiving is a holiday of celebrating,
giving thanks, loving, caring, and sharing.
It will always be the holiday
with all the enjoyment, the fun, and all
the delicious food.

Mandy
November 22, 1999

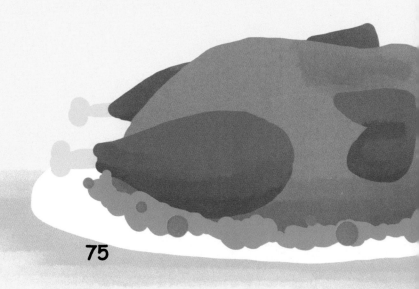

December

December is the month for wintertime.
It is the month we celebrate Christmas,
and Santa Claus brings all the good girls
and boys,
a big bagful of treats and toys.
In December, the angels like to watch
the snow fall.
Around Christmastime, the boys and girls
start hooraying as they hear
Santa's call.
Christmas is the holiday of the year
when Santa smells Christmas cookies
baking in the oven,
and hears the angels singing
Christmas carols as they pray.
December is the month that is cold enough for
cooking warm Christmas dinner,
and drinking a cup of hot chocolate
on Christmas Day.
Christmas is the holiday of loving, caring,
and sharing in every sweet way.
It is also the time of year when people
open presents.
The month of December puts smiles on
sweet faces,
and puts the love of Christmas in our
hearts while angels take
us to beautiful places.

A White Christmas

Winter is the coldest season of the year,
When we have a white Christmas
And celebrate all of the laughter and cheer.
As the snow falls, it is soft and white.
It falls out of the sky both day and night.
The holiday season is here when we have
A white Christmas.
On a white Christmas, we can open
Gifts during the holidays.
We are all in the Christmas spirit
Forever and always.
Decorating the Christmas tree is very,
Very nice as we celebrate on a cold,
Winter night,
And have a white Christmas so merry
And bright.

Mandy

When Angels Sing
A Christmas poem about celebrating the holidays

At Christmastime when angels sing,
they put all the love in our hearts
and the peace and the joy that
they bring.
When we celebrate Christmas, we
eat Christmas dinner, open gifts,
show each other we care.
Angels always sing beautiful Christmas
carols about the peace, joy, and love
that is always there.
We always think of Santa Claus as he sends
us Christmas gifts and treats on
Christmas Day.
When Angels sing, they hope and pray about
love in every precious way.
Christmas is the greatest holiday of the year
when the angels give warm hugs,
and warm hearts to strengthen their wings.
When they fly, they wish on all the beautiful
things.
We like to bake Christmas cookies for the
angels on Christmas Day with all the love
on their sweet faces,
and watch all the light shine bright in beautiful places.
The joy of Christmas will be celebrated for us
on a special day.
Christmas will always be a good holiday
for everyone when all the angels pray.

Mandy
November 22, 1999

Merry Christmas!!

78

Chapter 8

LOVE

I Love You xoxo

A Wedding Poem Presented To
Linda and Gary Delaune

With a man and a woman so deeply in love,
The sweet, loving couple will live
With the love, faith, and happiness
From above.
This wedding is full of the sweetest love
And the sweetest memories.
After Linda and Gary Delaune get married,
They will go away on a honeymoon
Full of hugs and kisses,
So sweet and true.

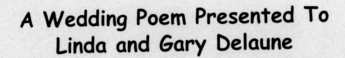

They will live happily ever after and cherish
The love that they share.
Both of these sweet people have hearts
So full of tender love and care.
Congratulations to these newlyweds,
As they live a sweet life together.
We wish them all the love and happiness.
So sweet and precious forever.

From their beloved best friend,
Miss Amanda Click

Getting Around And Getting Over You

Getting over you is like playing
a slow love song,
without breaking my heart and
making my tears fall.
I need you to love me and kiss me
all over again making love strong.
I can forget all of the doubts and
the fears,
and the problems that I've struggled
with for the last 22 years.
Getting around is hard to do
when I need your love.
I need to get over you like the sun shining
and the stars above.
My tears won't stop falling and
My heart won't stop breaking.
Getting over you will make my
heart stop aching.
I just can't go on without you.
I need to get around and get over you,
and make love sweet and true.
Getting over you is like loving you and
not letting my feelings drift away,

and getting over the hurt and pain
that used me everyday.
The bad things that tore me apart
gave me a cold, cold heart.
When you left me, I was down on my
my knees, begging to get
back to you.
When my eyes filled with tears, I
thought about the feelings that I
could never live through.
I could never sleep at night.
All I could do was cry into my pillow,
and hold you tight,
wishing you were there with me.
I need to get over you,
and get rid of the heartaches
that I could not handle.
All the tears I had to cry so much,
took away my sweet touch.
Now that I need you back,
getting over you will put
love back into my heart.
It will make me feel
better and will never
be apart.

March 5, 1999

I NEED YOU

I need you
Right now.
Because I woke up
This morning with
A headache
Thinking of you
You are very sweet,
And very kind.
That you will heal
My pain somehow
I was all cried out
Over the pain
That I needed
You!
You know that I
Love you
So much,
That whenever love
Hurts,
You are there for me.
To comfort me,
To hold me
In your arms
So that I can have your
Sweet, heartfelt
Touch.
Sometimes it's okay to
Cry.
If I am hurting
And you can wipe them
Away.

When Jesus talks to me
From heaven
Above.
You are always with
Me to make
It better
Each Day!
All that matters
To me,
Is that we love each
Other.
Whenever I need you,
You are so precious,
So kind
A part of me will always
Be with you, every day
When you are on
My mind!
I want you,
I need you,
And I am so in love with
You!
You just make my heart
Melt
And you are so sweet
And true!

TO: MATTHEW MOSELEY
FROM: MANDY CLICK
I LOVE YOU SO MUCH!

I'm Already Taken

I'm already taken, but I can only be
Your friend.
I understand that you want to go with me,
But I already have a boyfriend who
Will always love me and take care of me
Until the end.
I know that you feel kind of downhearted
Because you have no one to love,
But there is nothing that I can do about it.
You are my friend who is so friendly
Like the heavenly stars above.
Me and my sweetheart have known each other
For a long time,
And I don't know what I would do without him
By my side.
Even though I'm just your good friend,
I still have feelings for you and the rest of my friends
And I know how they feel inside.
My sweetheart gave me a promise ring this past year
For Christmas and it means so much
To me, friend.
Don't be sad, you will find someone to love
One sweet day.
You are still my friend with all of the warm
Hellos and friendly handshakes.
Friend, there is something that you need to know;

I would feel uncomfortable about going
With someone new,
And starting a new life with someone else
Would be hard to do.
I'm sorry that I'm already taken,
But I don't mind being your friend.
Having someone to love is such a sweet thing
When you are not single,
But I'm already taken to a sweet love
That keeps our hearts together.
Joking around with me is okay,
As long as you do it as a friend
In a very kind way.
I know that you want to go with me,
But there is nothing I can do.
I know that being single is a really heartbreaking
Thing,
But as long as I am your friend,
I can still try to open my heart,
Up to you.
Friend, I know that you are not so lucky
Without a girlfriend,
But you will find someone to love one day.
Even though I'm already taken,
I can still be your friend.

By: Amanda Click

I'M NEVER LETTING
YOU GO

When I look into your eyes,
I look into God's heart of love!
Your heart belongs to me when I
Hold you in my arms in heaven above!
I'm never letting you go,
Because my love for you is so strong,
More than you will ever know,
More than words can say!
I will never leave you behind,
You will always be on my mind,
Every beautiful night,
Every heavenly day!
If I ever have to go away,
It will be your sweet love
That I will miss,
Down on my knees, I will pray!
I promise that I will stay with you
So that I can feel your sweet kiss!
You're my light,
You're my love!
I'm never letter you go,
As long as the river runs to the sea,
Forever in my heart, you will always be
Under the beautiful sunshine
Thinking and dreaming so sweetly of me!

TO: MATTHEW JOSEPH MOSELEY!
FROM YOUR BEST FRIEND:
MANDY CLICK

In My Heart There Is A Love

In my heart, there is a love
always sweet and always forgiving
like the sunshine in heaven above.
Love will always be with me and stay with me
if I find it hard to breathe,
or when I need someone to pull me through.
My heart and soul is loved so deeply
inside of me when I need a warm, friendly hug.
A hug from a special friend,
who will take care of me until the end.
If I am feeling down, there are many friends
who will walk with me along the way,
to a heavenly love that will brighten my darkest days.
Love is a dream come true,
when I think of my friends who are so kind
and so gentle in the things they do.
My heart is full of an endless love that will last
forever,
and for always, with warm hugs, I will always have
friends who will stick together.
Having a friend in my heart is like having
a special bond of love.
A love like an angel in heaven above.
As long as I have faith, trust, and love,
there will always be an angel watching over me
and the beautiful things that I see.
My friends are the keys to my heart,
for always, with wings of love to fly.
They are my angels in heaven who will take
care of me if I need a hug.
All of the love in my heart will stay with me
and my friends forever, as the beautiful sun
shines in the clear, blue sky.

Mandy

Love Is Fragile, Love Is Blind

Love is so fragile,
that if we don't treat it right,
our hearts will break in two.

Love is so blind,
that if we don't have it strong in our hearts,
we can't make it last.

Love is so sensitive,
that if we forget about it,
it will upset us.

Love is so careful,
that if we don't keep it,
it will not put faith in us.

Love is fragile, Love is blind.
We will always be careful and treat it right,
and always keep it sweet and kind.

Mandy
June 24, 2000

Love Is In The Air

Love is in the air when you love,
dream, and care.
A heart is a symbol for love.
It is a feeling of happiness
from angels above.
When the sun is shining and
the sky is blue,
the love in your heart is so true.
The flowers grow beautifully,
and the wind blows peacefully.
The rain falls lightly,
and the night stars shine brightly.
When angels sweetly pray,
it makes love so sweet everyday.

Mandy
March 2, 1999

No Broken Hearts

There are no broken hearts,
no turning back,
no one to blame,
no hurting inside,
no teardrops falling,
no getting upset or crying,
no feeling sad,
or no sorrow or pain.
There is love so sweet and tender
in my heart.
Forever, this love will never be apart.
I had friends in the past who moved
far, far away.
I've really missed them in the last few years
day by day.
Right now there are no broken hearts,
no friendship problems,
no running away,
no bad days,
no hard feelings,
and no swearing.
I love the friends I have made now who
have feelings for me inside.
They have hearts to love, feelings to feel,
and wings to fly.
They will always be my angels shining like
diamonds in the sky.
I'm glad that there are no broken hearts,
no fights,
no arguments,
no telling secrets,
no stealing,
no taking advantage,
and no broken hearts.
My friends remind me as my pretty flowers
growing,
and they are my shining stars so beautiful
and bright,
in the light of the day and the dark of the night.

Mandy
January 16, 2000

Roses Are Red, Violets Are Blue

Roses are red, violets are blue. You are
my boyfriend who is so sweet and true.
Roses are red when you show your love to me.
Violets are blue when I look into your sweet
eyes that I see.
When I pick some flowers for you,
I put love into your heart
and like the sweet things you do.
Roses are red, violets are blue, You are
the one I love,
who has the prettiest blue eyes from heaven
above.
Roses are red when you dream of me in
every sweet way.
Violets are blue when you love, dream, and pray.
When I look at roses, I think about you,
and look at the sky that is as pretty as blue.
Roses are red, violets are blue, you are
the one who shows all your love and care,
when you give me all your hugs and kisses
that we share.
Roses are red when I put love into your heart
all day long.
Violets are blue when I sing a beautiful love song.
When I look at violets, I look at a pretty rainbow,
and hold you in my arms as the flowers grow.
Roses are red, violets are blue.
A sweet hug and kiss is my wish for you.

Mandy
"_____" I will always love you with
all my heart.
October 2, 1999

93

So Far Away

When you are so far away,
I always think of you,
and my heart will always
be there to stay.
I know you will come back
to me, but when you
are not here,
I will dream of your
love tonight.
I love you so much that
you are my beautiful light.
I don't want you to be so far
away,
because I will miss you day by day.
I know that you will never
leave me.
I want to look at your pretty eyes
that I see.
Your heart will always be full
of love.
I will never leave you or forget you.
You will be my sunshine above.
There are many times I do not
get to see you,
but when I see your face,
your love for me keeps me
warm and true.
When you are somewhere else
or in another place,
you are so far away and I
miss seeing your sweet face.

Mandy
March 1, 1999

The Ditched Ring I Will Treasure Forever

I received a special treasure
from my boyfriend who I will love forever.
It is a ring that will always be a piece of my heart.
As I wear this ring,
we will always stay together
and not be apart.
I'm so surprised that my sweetheart
found this ring for me.
With love in his heart,
the ring is the most beautiful thing.
When my boyfriend put this ring on my finger,
I got to thinking how it ended up in the ditch.
Then I gazed into his pretty eyes full of love,
and I was so happy that he found the lost ring
that I will treasure forever.
The ditched ring that I'm wearing
is precious,
is full of light,
and has a gemstone that is very bright.
My boyfriend just gave me all of his happiness
and a piece of his heart.
That was very sweet of him giving
me such a beautiful keepsake treasure
that I will keep on my finger forever.
With his heart so warm
so true,
and so full of love,
he gave me a beautiful ring.
that is really a precious thing.

The Roses

The roses are a symbol for love.
They are pretty like the angels
Above.
The roses are flowers that bloom
With love as they grow.
They let heaven's light shine
As they glow

Mandy

There You'll Be With Me

There you'll be with me in your sweet, gentle heart
That I adore.
With your beautiful blue eyes shining like the stars,
There you'll be in my heart forevermore.
Baby, when it is your smile that I see,
I will always keep you with me.
In my dreams,
I feel you making my heart melt,
And giving me the sweetest touch I have ever felt.
Your kisses are so romantic,
That they kiss the sky with a beautiful
Rainbow.
With my arms wrapped around you,
I will love you so.
There you'll be with me,
Whenever I need you by my side.
I can always talk to you about how I feel inside.
In my dreams,
I see you shine so beautifully in the sky.
I'm so happy to have you in my life,
And that you have wings of love to fly.
When you kiss me on your sweet lips,
You make my heart fill with love
In every way.
There you'll be with me,
In heaven above every sweet day.
Wherever I am,
You're right there for me.
In my dreams,
I see the moon shining on you
And feel my heart loving on you.
Baby, you are my soul and inspiration,
Now and forever.
We are the perfect pair who will alway
Stay together.
Baby, wherever I am,
You're right there for me.
Forever, with a beautiful river running to the sea,
There you'll be with me.

TO: MATTHEW JOSEPH MOSELEY

Hey sweetheart,
When I feel you
Holding me tight,
It makes me
Think of your first
Kiss from me
That I gave you last
Friday night!
As I laid me down to
Sleep,
On your
Shoulder,
It was a sweet
Precious moment
That we will
Forever keep!
I am so blessed to
Have you in my life,
Sweetheart,
That we will never
Let go,
Never break up
And never be
Apart.
Loving words
And the touch of
Your hand
Always help me
Put my troubles
Behind me!

With your loving arms
Around me,
I understand!
I will never let
Nothing happen to
Us,
My love!
You know how much
I love you
From the sweet heavens
Above!
What really warms
My heart
Is your first
Kiss,
Valentine!
When it is you
That I miss,
I think of you and
Your sweet
Loving heart
And forever
You are all
Mine!

Monday, January 21, 2019

FROM YOUR FRIEND.
MANDY CLICK!

I love you with a bushel and a peck
And a hug around the neck LOL

When I See You Smile

When I see you smile at me,
I see a beautiful light of love
as pretty as can be.
I see your pretty blue eyes shine.
Your smile is so pretty that
it makes you a sweetheart of mine.
Love makes you feel good
when you smile.
It makes a light in your eyes
that shine for a long while.
When I see you smile,
I think of all the sweet things
you do.
Forever in my heart, you will
always be sweet and true.

Mandy
March 2, 1999

You Are My Everything

You are my everything, and you
appreciate all of the love
and joy you bring.
You are my sunshine in the sky,
and my angel that flies high.
Your feelings show me how
sweet you kiss me,
and how nice we can be.
You are my one and only
true love,
in the bright heavens above.
You are my everything and
love that gives me light.
You are my stars in the sky
that shine bright.

Mandy

Your Love Is...

Your love is very sweet
for me,
when I kiss you.
Thinking of you everyday.
I always miss you.
You are as beautiful as a
pretty red rose
blooming in the sun
light,
and you are my stars
in the beautiful sky
that shine at night.
Your love is like a gentle
breeze blowing in
the wind
softly and slowly.
You are always in my
heart,
with your beautiful blue
eyes all aglow.
Honey, I just want to
say, in every sweet
way,
that I love you,
and that you are sweet and loving
in everything you
do.

From your girlfriend
Mandy Click

Chapter 9

NATURE

Nature

There is nothing like the sounds
of nature,
like the birds and the bees.
As they fly across the big blue sky,
they see all the beautiful flowers and the trees.
As the river gently runs to the sea,
the wind blows lightly,
like a nice summer breeze
blowing in the heavens so bright.
As the stars shine in the navy blue sky,
they shine down on all of earth's
beautiful things,
like the moon and the beautiful light
from heaven and the dark of night.
As the flowers bloom pretty petals,
they look beautiful as they grow,
like all the bright, green grass growing
in the meadow.
As the birds fly around the trees,
using their feathery wings,
they enjoy the nice, soothing sounds of nature,
like all of the other birds that sing.
As the bees fly around the pretty flowers,
they look for honey or nectar.
They like to look at the pretty flowers as
their petals show off their color so
beautiful and bright.
The nice, sweet, soothing sounds of nature
are like the birds, bees, flowers, and trees,
and all of angels who fly around heaven's
beautiful light.

January 8, 2000

Rain Makes A Flower Grow

Rain makes a flower grow with
love.
Love that is strong like a warm
hug and kiss.
A flower is the most beautiful thing
for an angel.
Flowers are a symbol for love,
friendship, and happiness.
Rain makes a flower grow
so pretty that love is
always there when
we need it.
Angels like picking the pretty
flowers, like roses, violets,
sunflowers, and daisies.
When rain makes them grow,
they are the love that
shines in the heavens.
Flowers are so beautiful
and they make everything
sparkle and shine.
As the wings of an angel glow,
and with the world's most
beautiful things,
rain makes a flower grow.

Amanda Click
June 20, 1999

105

Chapter 10

WEATHER

As Hurricane Ike Passes On
Bracing From A Fierceful Storm

We all try to stay calm
as Hurricane Ike passes on,
hoping it does
not damage our soul,
rip through our hearts,
and destroy our lives that
we hope will not be gone.
Bracing from Hurricane Ike,
will keep us safe from fear.
Feeling safe and secure
from this storm,
will keep our hearts strong
and help us not shed a tear.
With this fierceful storm
blowing through,
and the gloomy sky dumping
numerous amounts of rain,
the good Lord will be with us,
take our hand,
and save us from pain.
With the wind blowing hard
through the goodness

of mother nature,
all empty and alone,
the angels are praying for mercy
and are making sure we feel
safe,
and will not be left out on our
own.
Without the good Lord,
how could we survive?
How could we breathe
with no air?
We are all thankful that
we will be okay
from fierceful Hurricane Ike
that was trying to take us
all away.
When it is all over with,
there will come a beautiful
day
that will always be there.

By: Mandy Click

Written on September 13, 2008
The same day Hurricane Ike hit.
Rewritten on May 1, 2009.

When The Rain Falls

When the rain falls from the sky,
It falls from the gray clouds
That look gloomy from up high.
The rain falls as it melts the warm sunshine
Away,
And with the thunder rolling and the lighting
Striking,
It is such a stormy day.
The rain makes the grass turn a pretty summer
Green,
And makes the pretty flowers grow everywhere.
Wherever there are stormy clouds,
Rain is always there.
Little drops of water falling from the dark, gray
Sky
Are called raindrops.
It dampens all of the trees, grass, flowers,
And all the wonder of nature
When it stops.
When the lightning strikes,
It light up in the lonely dark of night,
And lights up the gray clouds,
Very bright.
At night, as the dark gray clouds cover the moon,
There will be a thunderstorm coming real soon.
In the daytime as the gray clouds cover the blue sky
And the sun,
It starts pouring down rain.
The thunder and lightning starts rumbling
As a thunder comes through,
And makes the leaves and flowers wilt
With drops of dew.
Rain and thunderstorms
are the most frightening type of weather
In those gray rain clouds
That light up through the sky.
Rain is like teardrops falling from a sad face.
If there is rain,
There sure will be a stormy place.

Wintertime

It's the time of the year
when we keep our hearts
warm
in front of the fire.
Keeping ourselves near and
dear in the
cold,
we all have each other to
have and to hold.
The bitter, cold snow falling
from the sky
is a beautiful scenery of
white snowflakes falling from
up high.
Cozying up to a soft, warm
blanket in the wintertime
and a cup of hot chocolate
will melt our hearts.
Friends always get together on
a cold winter's day or night
and stay cozy in the nice
warm light.
Having friends by our side,
friends who will always
be there in the wintertime,
Keeps all of us
warm in the season that is
very cold,
but leaving us with kindness,
warmth, and care.

Mandy Click
January 18, 2010

A Note from the Editor

I have earned two (2) black belts during my lifetime – one in success and the other one in failure. The first inception or "idea" of the East Texas Fun Bunch (ETFB) was in 2006, the year my Mom died. It came from my desire to provide my younger sister, Betsy Elaine Burke, the same love and support that my Mom had given to her throughout her life. Betsy was born in 1950 with Down Syndrome. ETFB grew, evolved and changed – just like this book did.

I am so grateful and happy for the people and organizations that I met along the way – those that were supportive as well as those that were not – they both provided invaluable learning lessons and assisted me in growing a larger and stronger heart, forgiveness (toward myself and others), persistence, resiliency, resourcefulness and creativity. Without each person and event along the way, I would not be the person I am today. So below is my tribute to all of YOU:

First and foremost, I want to thank God – my Higher Power – my divine and infinite source of love and wisdom.

My parents, Anna Belle and Ward R. Burke, who gave Barbara, Betsy and me the greatest gift of all – LIFE!

All the many amazing, awesome, beautiful (inside and out) special friends of Betsy that I had the honor and pleasure of being with and sharing quality time.

Then, in addition to the people that Mandy acknowledged on page iv, the following is a partial list (in alphabetical order according to first letter). Each of these people and/or organizations had a significant role in my personal evolution through ETFB, Inc. and/or editing and publishing this book and/or through personal relationships.

112

A. William "Bill" Benitez; A-1 Party Rentals of Lufkin; Aaron Smith; Aimee Slusher and staff at Skelton Slusher Barnhill Watkins Wells PLLC; Amy Wych; Angelina College, Angelina Arts Alliance and Community Services staff, including Karen McBee, Michael J. Simon, Robert Lee (deceased, taught computer classes), Susan Rangel, Timothy Ditoro and others; Anita Milam; Barbara Burke Smith; Ben Smith and family; Brookshire Brothers; Burke, Board of Trustees, faculty and staff, and particularly Carolyn McDonald, Deidra Davis, Jake Squires, Lisa May, Stephanie Yates, and Tammy Forney; BXS Insurance; Camp for All; Carla Arnold, Service Director and the staff at Oak Creek Center/Day Hab/Vocational; Carolyn Chalender; Charlene Warren; Chris Sanford; Christine Huynh and family; Christopher Wong and family; Connie L. Murphy (consultant for this book); Crown Colony Country Club; CVG Graphics (Eric Chinn and Sid Shanks); Dana Conley; Davis/Higgineotham Insurance, Inc.; Deloise G. Vasquez; Destin Sabani; Dill relatives; Edunjobi Oluwaseun (Lagos, Nigeria); Elton L. Foster; Everett Lunning, Jr.; First Bank & Trust East Texas (now called Southside Bank); Gary and Tracy Lee and family; Grace Ann Wilson; Jaime West; Janet Thomas; Jean Pachicano; Jo Whitaker; John P. Friesen, Jr. and the Evergreen Group at RBC Wealth Management; Katie Bowers; Linda Wright; Lindsey Hines; Lisa Crow; Lori Lamb and staff at Axley & Rode LLP; Lufkin Daily News; Lufkin Printing Company and staff; Lynn Fisher; Lynn Hopper and staff at Lufkin State Supported Living Center; Marilyn "Mimi" Pruitt Duncan; Marsha Ford, Tiffany Shultz (Moore-Rich) and the staff at St. Giles Living Center, Inc.; Mary Morrissey and staff at DreamBuilderLive.com/marilyn88; Merri Nichols and family; Museum of East Texas; Patricia and Vernon Evans; Patricia King and the staff at EduCare Community Living; Patricia Warner; Peyton Walters; PineCrest Retirement Community and staff; Pineywoods Foundation; Pineywoods Jamboree; Remi Bryant; Restoration Bistro; RSVP; Sandra Jo Tucker; Simon and Louise Henderson Foundation; T.L.L. Temple Foundation and staff; Tara Watson-Watkins and staff at the Lufkin Convention and Visitors Bureau; Tom Darmstadter; Trey Moore with Morgan Insurance Agency; Upwork.com and their freelancers; Vickie Evans; Wayne Haglund; Wyatt Leinart and Trustees

Please forgive me if I inadvertently left out your name.

With Heartfelt Joy and Appreciation to each one of you,

Marilyn Ruth Burke, Austin, Texas

Thanks!

God bless you!

114

Thanks!
God bless you!

Poetry in Motion

Amanda Gail Click
"Mandy"

Angelina College
3500 S 1st St
Lufkin, Texas 75901-7328

Angelina College
Scholarship Fund
P.O. Box 1768
Lufkin, Texas 75902-1768

— —

To make an envelope:

Please tear this page out of the book.

Fold the paper in $\frac{1}{2}$ along the dotted line.

Place your check inside the envelope.

Make check payable to Angelina College.

In the Memo Section, please write:

ETFB Scholarship Fund.

Use clear, Scotch tape to seal the three (3) open sides.

Do NOT use staples.

Place a stamp in top right corner.

Thanking you in advance for your generosity.